Generations

Three One Act Plays

by

Stephen Evans

Morey Norkin

Michael Gilles

"All diseases run into one, old age."
Ralph Waldo Emerson

This is a work of fiction. The names, characters, places, and incidents are either the products of the author's imagination or are used fictitiously, and any resemblance to actual persons living or dead, business establishments, events, or locales is entirely coincidental.

For production permissions and rights, contact: info@istepheneavans.com

Monuments Copyright © 2019 by Stephen Evans. All rights reserved.

Last Laugh Copyright © 2019 by Morey Norkin. All rights reserved.

Late Nights in Cars Copyright © 2019 by Michael Gilles. All rights reserved.

Book Layout ©2017
BookDesignTemplates.com

Generations: 1st Edition

ISBN: 978-1-7345135-8-5

Contents

Monuments 1
Last Laugh 52
Late Nights in Cars 87
Acknowledgements 113
About the Playwrights 115

GENERATIONS

Monuments

by

Stephen Evans

Cast of Characters

WALDO   Ralph Waldo Emerson, age 69

NELLY   Emerson's Daughter Ellen, age 33[1], referred to as Nelly in this play because the playwright was getting confused.

ELLEN   Emerson's first wife, Ellen, age 21

Scene

A boat on the Nile River.

Time

1873.

.

---

[1] May be played by the same actress.

Act I Scene 1

Setting: Emerson's cabin. Downstage right is a desk, chair behind, so the actor faces the audience. Up left is a doorway. Downstage from that is a window of sorts.

At **Rise**: WALDO is at his desk. He is struggling to light an oil lamp.

WALDO
Let there be light.

NELLY
(From offstage)
Papa, you should come out on deck. You can see the pyramids.

WALDO
I imagine they will last until the return trip.

(Nelly enters.)

NELLY
What are you working on, Papa?

WALDO
Genesis.

(She laughs.)

NELLY
Can you be more specific?

WALDO
Chapter 1, verse 3.

(He fiddles with the lamp.)

NELLY
Are you writing about it?

WALDO
No, I am re-enacting it.

(He fiddles some more, without success, then throws up his hands.)

WALDO
Let there be light!

(She moves to the desk and lights the lamp for him.)

NELLY
There. Now you can call the light day.

MONUMENTS

WALDO
(Squinting)
I would call this dim not day.

NELLY
And set about dividing the darkness from the light.

WALDO
Wishful thinking, daughter.

NELLY
As you have always done, Papa.

(She kisses his forehead and looks at the desk.)

NELLY
What are you working on today instead of talking a stroll on deck with your devoted daughter?

WALDO
Plutarch's Morals. I wish Henry were here. He knew the Greeks so much better than I.

(Ellen is struck with sadness, her brilliant father's decline brought home again, as it is many times each day.)

NELLY
He is gone, Papa. Henry Thoreau died ten years ago.

(Waldo stops, confused and then struggles to remember, accepts, then tries to cover his struggle. Nelly, ever the loving daughter, waits patiently for his mind to catch up.)

WALDO

Then I change my mind. I don't wish he were here. He would be annoyed with me for disturbing his lecture to the Almighty.

(Nelly laughs, but the sadness shows through.)

NELLY

You are a wise man.

(Waldo, all too aware of his decline, smiles.)

WALDO

So everyone tells me.

NELLY

Do you doubt it, O Sage of Concord?

WALDO

Among many things.

(Nelly tries to change the subject.)

NELLY

I thought Plutarch was a Roman.

WALDO
No. He was a citizen of the Empire, but he was Greek by birth, and by thought.

NELLY
Plutarch was one of my favorites as a child. When you were away on your speaking tours, I would sneak into your study and read him.

WALDO
You were a precocious child. I credit your mother with that. I was away so often. Did you read the Lives?

NELLY
No. Too stuffy, too many wars. I liked the Morals actually. Is this Professor Goodwin's translation?

WALDO
Yes. Saved from the fire. I am to write the introduction and must have it ready soon.

(Again, the sadness hits her. She gathers herself and crosses back to the desk, and lays her hand on his shoulder with great tenderness.)

NELLY
That is already done, Papa.

(She turns to the front of the book.)

NELLY

(Reading)

With an introduction by Ralph Waldo Emerson.

(Waldo looks at the book, confused. He turns a few pages. Then turns a few back, always the familiar struggle to comprehend, catch up with the world.)

WALDO

It is done.

(Another pause.)

Wonderful!

(He relaxes.)

Oh I am quite relieved. I was dreading the labor. The words do not flow as easily these days.

(He shakes it off, returning to a familiar quotation to explain the lapse.)

But who cares? As soon as we walk out of doors, Nature transcends all poets so far, that a little more or less skill in whistling is of no account.[2]

(Nelly understands, glances outside, then at him, and takes charge, as she has so often and will continue to do for the rest of his life.)

---

[2] From a letter to Caroline Sturgis, Oct. 23, 1857

                    NELLY
Papa, come out of this stuffy cabin and we'll find
chairs in the sun and watch the ages float past us.

   *(He smiles at her, grateful for her concern
   and her care.)*

   (The smile fades.)

   *(He looks around the cabin, again deep in
   confusion.)*

                    WALDO
This is a boat.

                    NELLY
Yes, Papa.

   (Waldo tries to solve the puzzle.)

                    WALDO
Not on the ocean.

                    NELLY
No.

                    WALDO
A river?

                    NELLY
Yes.

WALDO
A river.

NELLY
Yes.

(He looks out the window.)

WALDO
The Concord?

NELLY
No.

WALDO
No. Too large. Nor the Charles either.

NELLY
It is the Nile.

(Pause.)

WALDO
The Nile?

NELLY
We are in Egypt, Papa. We are sailing down the Nile on a boat named the Aurora. Remember how shocked we were at the price? Eight dollars a day.

(Slowly it dawns and he catches up.)

WALDO
Yes. I remember now. Can we afford such extravagance?

(She puts a hand on his shoulder.)

NELLY
We can. Remember the fire?

WALDO
The fire. Yes! The fire.

NELLY
The fire burned our house.

WALDO
Yes. Yes. Our poor home.

NELLY
Then your friends and so many admirers raised the money to send us on this trip while it is restored.

(He is lost in thought for a moment. Then he notices the book in front of him and turns back to it, something solid he understands.)

WALDO
According to Plutarch, the Egyptians invented horticulture.

NELLY
And slavery.

WALDO
The Egyptians did not invent slavery. They merely perfected it.

NELLY
That I thought was an American accomplishment.

WALDO
Now, now. Mr. Lincoln fixed all that.

NELLY[3]
Papa, surely you don't think--

(She sees him smiling.)

Yes, you know me well.

(Nelly picks up the volume, flips through.)

NELLY
I loved these stories. Especially...

(She finds the one she wants)

Isis and Osiris. I used to read this one over and over.

WALDO
That is hardly a story for children!

---

[3] Ellen, her mother Lidian, Henry Thoreau, and about half of Concord were staunch abolitionists and initially supporters of John Brown. Emerson, though not as personally passionate, sometimes lent his famous name to the cause.

NELLY[4]

Exactly why I loved it! It is the oldest love story in the world. Osiris was entombed by Typhon and thrown into the sea and Isis searched all over the world for him and opened the coffin and took out the body and laid her cheek against his and then Typhon found the body and cut it up into pieces and threw it into the Nile and Isis searched the river and found every piece except—

WALDO

Yes. Yes. I know the story.

NELLY

For a young girl, it was scandalous. And very romantic.

(Waldo gazes out the window.)

WALDO

It happened here, if it happened. Thousands of years ago. The tomb of Osiris is on the island of—

NELLY

Philae[5].

---

[4] Ellen never married, living in her father's house for the rest of her life, an adoring aunt to her sibling's children.
[5] Pronounced Fi-Lee

WALDO
Philae, which lies...

NELLY
Not far ahead of us.

> *(Philae reminds Waldo of something. He starts to drift away into memory.)*

WALDO
I have wanted to see Philae for many years.

NELLY
The captain tells me that the Wards are there, with Clover Adams[6].

WALDO
Many many years.

NELLY
I arranged transportation for us on Philae so we may join them straightaway.

> *(He pauses, then comes back. He turns to Nelly, takes her hands, and looks at her approvingly.)*

---

[6] Wife of Henry Adams and the inspiration for some of Henry James characters.

WALDO
You remind me of your mother, Ellen.

(She brushes the white hair away from his forehead.)

NELLY
I was named for her, Papa. But your first wife Ellen was not my mother.

(He laughs.)

WALDO
I am forgetful now I know. But that I have not forgotten. Your mother Lidian is the best woman, the best wife. She deserves...she deserves...you. You should be home helping her restore our home, not running away to foreign lands with your old Papa.

(Waldo stares at his hands.)

NELLY
Don't think of that now. There will be time enough for setting things right when we return home. If mother and Edith have not already done so.

WALDO
If anyone can, it is...Lidian. She is...the best woman, the best wife.

NELLY
Papa?

WALDO
Yes?

NELLY
I often wonder...

WALDO
As do I. In the blood I suppose. The wandering wondering Emersons.

NELLY
I often wonder, I was saying.

WALDO
If you are saying, you might as well say.

NELLY
I often wonder how you managed to convince Mother to name me after your first wife. And not just one name. She was Ellen Tucker Emerson. I am Ellen Tucker Emerson.

WALDO
You have wondered that?

NELLY
Can you blame me?

WALDO
I suppose not. Best ask your mother.

NELLY
I have. She said to ask you.

WALDO
Did she?

NELLY
She did. I think she was curious what your answer would be.

WALDO
So am I.

NELLY
I would like to know. If you remember.

WALDO
While I remember, you mean.

NELLY
You must have been quite persuasive. Even for Ralph Waldo Emerson.

WALDO
I suppose it was my idea. Back then I had that much audacity, and that little understanding of women. But your mother agreed.

NELLY
Apparently. But why?

WALDO

My first wife and I were married not even two years before she died, and she was ill with the consumption so much of that. I think we knew before we married.

NELLY

Knew what?

WALDO

That we had not much time.

> *(He is lost in thought again. Then, again, returns to the book.)*

WALDO

I wish Henry were here. He knew the Greeks so much better than I.

> *(Nelly sighs.)*

NELLY

I shall be on deck, Papa, riddling the sphinx. Join me.

> *(Nelly exits.)*

WALDO

One monument to another, eh?

> *(He continues to turn pages, then finally finds what he wants.)*

WALDO
(*Reading*)
With an introduction by Ralph Waldo Emerson.

(*He turns a few pages.*)

WALDO
(*Reading*)
Plutarch's popularity will return in rapid cycles. If over-read in this decade, so that his anecdotes and opinions become commonplace, and to-day's novelties are sought for variety, his sterling values will presently recall the eye and thought of the best minds, and his books will be reprinted and read anew by coming generations. And thus Plutarch will be perpetually rediscovered from time to time as long as books last.[7]

(*He closes the book.*)

WALDO
It is finished. I didn't know. I didn't remember. But how can one know what has been forgotten? Is there some sign? An empty space where memories used to be? Like a piece missing from a puzzle? I

---

[7] *Plutarch's Morals, with an Introduction by Ralph Waldo Emerson*

would like to know what I don't know. Even if that is the only thing I can know.

> *(He opens the book again, turns the pages more and more rapidly, almost desperately, then finally finds what he wants.)*

WALDO
(Reading)
And in the first place where she could take rest, and found herself to be now at liberty and alone, she opened the ark, and laid her cheeks upon the cheeks of Osiris, and embraced him and wept bitterly[8].

ELLEN (O.S.)
We knew.

> *(This voice. He can almost remember it.)*

WALDO
We knew?

---

[8] *Of Isis and Osiris*, Plutarch's Morals

ELLEN (O.S.)
That we had not much time.

(More familiar.)

WALDO
Did we?

ELLEN (O.S.)
We spoke of it.

(Waldo closes the book. He knows, but cannot believe.)

WALDO
I do not believe in the immortality of the individual soul.

ELLEN (O.S.)
Since when?

(He stands. The light grows around him.)

WALDO
Since I lost you.

(He turns upstage. Ellen is revealed upstage, wearing her funeral dress. Her face is covered by a veil.)

ELLEN
You never lost me.

WALDO
I couldn't find you.

ELLEN
It's not the same.

WALDO
Nothing is.

ELLEN
Nothing is.

(Ellen crosses down into the light.)

ELLEN
Anyway I'm not a ghost or a spirit or a lost soul. I'm a memory.

WALDO
Well then I suppose you can stay. There is plenty of room. Most of the other memories have left. And they took yesterday with them.

ELLEN
You haven't forgotten me, have you, Waldo? Have you forgotten your Ellinelli? Your Lady Frolick? Lady Pensero? Have you forgotten your queen, my king?

WALDO
Facts fade. Feelings remain.

ELLEN
You can't have forgotten everything. Else I would not be here.

WALDO
How can one know?

ELLEN
A puzzle. But then you like puzzles.

WALDO
Do I?

ELLEN
I hope so. I am one.

(She laughs. He smiles at the sound.)

WALDO
That is familiar.

ELLEN
Shall I remind you?

WALDO
Yes. Remind me. Please. Re<u>mind</u> me.

ELLEN
We met on Christmas day. You were my favorite gift. I was a woman of 16 and you were a boy of 24. We spoke of Byron. You thought I meant the poet and I thought you meant my spaniel. We were very confused for a moment, and then then your stern and serious ministerial face crinkled up and you laughed and laughed. And I decided then and there that you would marry me.

WALDO
You had a dog named Byron. I thought that was funny.

ELLEN
That you remember! I would be insulted but he was a very good dog.

WALDO
Byron.

ELLEN
A year later you brought me a book called *Forget Me Not*. A year! Now that is funny.

WALDO
That is ironic. It's not the same.

ELLEN
What is ironic is that I grew up in Concord, New Hampshire, and after I died you settled in Concord, Massachusetts.

WALDO
That is not ironic. It is a coincidence, and possibly a metaphor.

ELLEN
I wanted to be a poet and you wanted to be a minister. You ended up a poet and I ended up a memory. What is that?

WALDO
That is a tragedy.

ELLEN
Oh, your poetry is not that bad.

(He looks at her.)

WALDO
That is funny.

(She curtseys.)

ELLEN
Are they coming back?

WALDO
What?

ELLEN

The memories.

WALDO

Oh they come back occasionally. They just don't stay. Memories are like some old aunt who goes in and out of the house, and occasionally recites anecdotes of old times and persons which I recognize as having heard before, and she being gone again I search in vain for any trace.[9]

ELLEN

That sounds like something you wrote.

WALDO

I don't recall.

ELLEN

Shall I?

WALDO

What?

ELLEN

Stay?

(He looks offstage where Nelly has exited.)

WALDO

Ellen is...out there.

---

[9] *Essay on Memory*, Emerson

ELLEN
I am Ellen.

WALDO
You are Ellinelli. You are Lady Frolick and Lady Pensero.

ELLEN
I believe so.

WALDO
I have remembered something that I have forgotten.

ELLEN
You had forgotten but now you remember?

WALDO
No, I remember that I have forgotten.

ELLEN
I see.

WALDO
I have tried and tried.

ELLEN
Yes?

WALDO
For some time, I have tried.

ELLEN

Yes?

WALDO

I cannot recall.

ELLEN

Say it.

WALDO

Your face. I cannot recall your face.

ELLEN

Is that all?

WALDO

I want to. Very much. But I cannot.

ELLEN

I'm almost glad. I was not so beautiful toward the end. So pale and thin.

WALDO

You were always beautiful.

ELLEN

But wait. You have my miniature still?

WALDO

Your picture. Yes. I have it in my study. Or I did. Who knows where it is now? I don't think it burned. Though that night was so confusing.

ELLEN
Poor Waldo.

WALDO
That I remember. You called me that often.

ELLEN
If you have the miniature, then you can't have forgotten how I looked.

WALDO
I look at the painting. Often. But I do not recognize you when I see it.

ELLEN
Was it not a good likeness?

WALDO
It's not that. It just doesn't feel the same.

ELLEN
The same?

WALDO
As when I looked at you. I still remember the way I felt. Transcendent.

ELLEN
Transcendent? You make me sound very grand.

WALDO
You were.

ELLEN

Transcendent? No. I was a girl in love, for the first and only time. You mistake transcendent for incandescent.

(Her lighting brightens a bit)

WALDO

Transcendent sounds better.

ELLEN

You're just used to it[10].

WALDO

Perhaps.

ELLEN

I suppose I was a little transcendent, towards the end. It was so hard to hold on to life. I tried, for you.

WALDO

You were brave. I remember that.

ELLEN

We had so little time. I didn't want to waste it in tears.

---

[10] Emerson was the founder of American Transcendentalism.

WALDO
And your cough. Your terrible cough. And the blood. So much blood from such a tiny body.

ELLEN
I am healed now.

WALDO
I took you south, to try the climate.

ELLEN
To Philadelphia!

WALDO
And I had to leave you there and return to Boston. I have never felt so alone.

ELLEN
I was the one in Philadelphia.

WALDO
And I was desperate to know if you missed me as much as I missed you.

ELLEN
That is natural. You were so young.

WALDO
Natural. You were young. Was I ever young?

ELLEN
You were. You just didn't know it.

WALDO
I feel younger now, with you here.

ELLEN
Dear Waldo.

WALDO
Dear Waldo. I remember that, now, too. No one else has ever called me that. Lidian calls me Mr. Emerson. May I speak of her to you?

ELLEN
Sweet Waldo.

WALDO
I know she has never called me that. Not in my hearing anyway.

ELLEN
You love her.

WALDO
It is, imprecise, to use the same word for what I felt for you, and what I feel for her. But it is the only word we are given. Even Shakespeare never found another. So I suppose we must make do.

ELLEN

But this dream of love, though beautiful, is only one scene in our play. In the procession of the soul from within outward, it enlarges its circles ever, like the pebble thrown into the pond, or the light proceeding from an orb.[11]

WALDO

That sounds like something I once wrote.

ELLEN

It is.

WALDO

If you are a memory, how is it that you know something I wrote years after.

ELLEN

Memories don't abide alone. We coexist.

WALDO

Really?

ELLEN

Oh yes. We speak to one another often.

---

[11] *Essay on Love,* Emerson

WALDO

Memories speak to memories. That puts Homer in a different light.[12]

(Ellen laughs)

ELLEN

Speak, Memory—Of the cunning hero.

WALDO

The wanderer, blown off course time and again.

ELLEN

Well, think of it. What else is there to do but speak to each other? Especially when you spend so little time with us. Such a busy important man, always running around giving speeches.

WALDO

Lectures, not speeches. Politicians give speeches.

(She sticks her tongue out at him through the veil, laughs, spinning away, her white dress flowing around her. She stops, then turns slyly back to Waldo.)

ELLEN

In fact, Lidian and I have spoken.

---

[12] The beginning of the Odyssey.

WALDO
Pardon?

ELLEN
Lidian. Your second wife. You member her, don't you?

WALDO
Oh yes.

ELLEN
I thought so. Lidian and I have had long conversations.

WALDO
About me?

ELLEN
Oh yes!

WALDO
Oh no.

ELLEN
And she does also call you poor Mr. Emerson, if that is any consolation.

WALDO
For a memory, you are very chatty.

ELLEN
Memories are not miniatures.

WALDO
What are they? I don't remember.

ELLEN
Memory is a presumption of a possession of the future. Now we are halves, we see the past but not the future, but in that day will the hemisphere complete itself and foresight be as perfect as aftersight.[13]

WALDO
Or as imperfect. Did I write that?

ELLEN
Of course.

WALDO
It is like your face. Though I know it, I don't recognize it.

ELLEN
I like that one especially. It reminds me of your sermons. One of the saddest parts of being sick was that I could not attend your sermons.

WALDO
It reminds you?

---

[13] *Essay on Memory*, Emerson

ELLEN
You were so grand in the pulpit with your high cloak and sweet voice. And only once per sermon would you let yourself sneak a glance at your Ellinelli. And when you did look on my face, only for a second and with no smile or nod or sign, I knew I needed no other communion.

WALDO
Nor I.

(He turns suddenly.)

WALDO
I remember!

(Ellen turns away.)

ELLEN
My face?

WALDO
For a year afterwards, I walked each day to your grave.

(He turns to her.)

ELLEN
Poor Waldo.

WALDO
You asked me to.

ELLEN
Did I?

WALDO
Breathe not yet, but wait until
My spirit is set free.
Then whisper round my grave
The tale of my release —[14]

ELLEN
I wrote that.

WALDO
You did.

ELLEN
And you remember.

WALDO
I do.

ELLEN
But you cannot recall my face.

WALDO
No. I remember I walked each day to your grave.

(He takes a step toward her.)

---

[14] *To the South Wind*, Ellen Emerson

WALDO
I needed to see your face. Once more.

(Another step. Dimmer.)

WALDO
Just once more.

(Another step, and he is near her.)

WALDO
One day I entered your tomb.

(She turns to him.)

WALDO
And opened the coffin.

(He reaches up to her veil.)

WALDO
And I saw.

(Her light goes out. He lowers his arm.)

WALDO
Nothing.

ELLEN
Nothing?

WALDO
Nothing.

ELLEN
It was empty?

WALDO
We were in darkness.

ELLEN
That is natural.

WALDO
Natural. Yes. Does it bother you?

ELLEN
What?

WALDO
That I, came to see you?

ELLEN
I often come to see you.

WALDO
Are you sure you are not a ghost?

ELLEN
Maybe a memory is a ghost that lives inside us.

WALDO
Maybe a ghost is a memory that lives outside us.

ELLEN
But you don't believe in the immortality of the soul.

WALDO
Maybe that is where memories go. The afterlife belongs not to us but to them.

(She steps into the light again.)

ELLEN
Perhaps they are us.

WALDO
After you died, I resigned from the ministry. Your inheritance paid for long trip through Europe. I was lost, so I thought I may as well be lost somewhere new.

ELLEN
Clever Waldo.

WALDO
That's a new one. I wandered for a year. Syracuse. Naples. Rome. Florence. Paris. London.

ELLEN
So far from home.

WALDO
Without you I had no home.

ELLEN
So far then.

WALDO
I met great writers that I had admired: Landor, Coleridge, Wordsworth, Carlyle.

ELLEN
Your Heroes.

WALDO
I found them to be...just men. Poor men. Flawed men.

ELLEN
You were disappointed.

WALDO
Yes. But. It is a kind of freedom, to learn what is possible, and by whom.

ELLEN
It is.

WALDO
By the end I knew something in me had changed, but I did not know what.

ELLEN
I know.

WALDO
I came back, to Concord. I could not return to Boston and the church.

ELLEN
I understand.

WALDO
I had to make a living, so I started writing, and speaking.

(She smiles.)

ELLEN
Lecturing.

(And he smiles.)

WALDO
Lecturing. I married Lidian.

ELLEN
A good woman.

WALDO
A good woman.

ELLEN
You needed her.

WALDO
I loved her. Love her. You can tell her I said so.

ELLEN
You can tell her.

WALDO
I can tell her.

ELLEN
She gave you children.

WALDO
Ellen. Edith. Edward. Poor Waldo, gone so young.[15]

ELLEN
Poor Waldo. So much tragedy.

WALDO
So much life.

ELLEN
If I had not gotten sick…

WALDO
I could not have left you.

ELLEN
Maybe that is why I had to leave you.

WALDO
Let us build altars to the Beautiful Necessity.[16]

---

[15] Emerson's son Waldo died of scarlet fever at age five.
[16] *Essay on Experience*, Emerson

ELLEN
Though thou loved her as thyself,
As a self of purer clay,
Though her parting dims the day,
Stealing grace from all alive; [17]

WALDO
Heartily know,
When half-gods go,
The gods arrive. [17]

ELLEN
It's all right.

WALDO
I remember.

ELLEN
The loving. And the leaving. It is all right.

WALDO
Silent rushes the swift Lord
Through ruined systems still restored,
Broad-sowing, bleak and void to bless,
Plants with worlds the wilderness,
Waters with tears of ancient sorrow
Apples of Eden ripe to-morrow;
House and tenant go to ground.[18]

---

[17] *Give All to Love*, poem, Emerson
[18] *Threnody*, poem, Emerson

ELLEN
Lost in God.[18]

WALDO
In Godhead found.[18]

(He returns to the desk.)

WALDO
I have wondered from time to time what my last memory will be. After all the others have escaped me. What will be the last? Like Pandora's box, my mind will shut tight, yet one will tap on the lid and cry out 'wait! I am still here.' Will it be you? Lidian? Nelly? Henry? Little Waldo feverish in the bed? What will it be? What part of myself will be the last to say goodbye?

ELLEN
It may be a bit selfish but I should like it to be me. But it won't be.

(She starts to exit.)

ELLEN
It won't be me. Or Lidian. Or Nelly. Or Henry. Or little Waldo. For you it will be a boat on river in a land where history waits.

####WALDO
I have lived two lives. One of the mind. One of the heart. The mind is leaving. Only the heart remains.

(She turns back to him. He looks at her.)

####WALDO
One monument to another.

(The light slowly fades.)

THE END

The History

In July of 1872, Ralph Waldo Emerson's house in Concord, Massachusetts, caught fire. His many friends and admirers raised money for repairs, and to send him on a journey across the ocean while those repairs were being made. He was accompanied on the voyage by his daughter, Ellen Tucker Emerson, who was named for his first wife.

At the time of this voyage, Emerson was one the most famous Americans, and certainly the most famous intellectual since Franklin. Everywhere he went he was invited to speak and read from his works. But his mind, which has been declining for a few years, declined even more seriously after the fire. No longer considered capable of traveling alone, his daughter accompanied him and managed the trip.

This tale of a few moments on that voyage is imagined, though based in some details on the letters of Emerson's first wife Ellen and his namesake daughter Ellen, and his journals.

MONUMENTS

Emerson's journal for March 29, 1832, lists a quote from Aristotle and this cryptic single line:

> *I visited Ellen's tomb & opened the coffin.*

Bibliography

Plutarch:

The Morals, by Plutarch, corrected and revised by William W. Goodwin, Ph. D. 1870

Emerson Biographies (my favorites among many):

Emerson: The Mind on Fire by Robert D. Richardson Jr.

Ralph Waldo Emerson by Oliver Wendell Holmes Sr.

Emerson Correspondence:

Letters of Ellen Tucker Emerson, edited by Edith W. Gregg

Letters of Ralph Waldo Emerson, edited by Ralph L. Rusk

One First Love, The Letters of Ellen Luisa Tucker to Ralph Waldo Emerson, edited by Edith W. Gregg

Emerson Works:

Most of Emerson's own works are in print and/or available online.

MONUMENTS

Last Laugh

By

Morey Norkin

Cast of Characters

JACKIE Jewish comic, 70ish, never made the big-time

JENNIFER Comic, 30ish

Scene

Dressing room backstage at a comedy club.

Time

2010 or thereabouts.

Act I Scene 1

Setting:: A makeup table and mirror. A few chairs. A futon/sofa. Bottles of water or water dispenser.

At Rise:: JENNIFER is pacing around the dressing room. She flips through index cards as she paces..

(She suddenly stops center. Delivers monologue directly to audience.

JENNIFER

Relationships are so difficult. I tried speed dating recently. You know, where you talk to someone for a couple of minutes and if there's no connection, you just move on to the next person? Kind of a microcosm of my dating history. It was like all the terrible dates and relationships I've ever had were all gathered in one spot. Like The Bachelorette from hell. There they all were: the losers, abusers, control freaks, closeted gays... and then there was someone different. A sweet face, twinkling eyes... I said you seem so different from the rest of these guys. You have a nice aura. What's your name? He said, "Jeffrey Dahmer. But don't worry, I'm vegan!"

> *(To herself)*

I hope that's edgy enough. I wish they hadn't told me they were expecting an SNL producer tonight.

> *(She sits at the makeup mirror nervously adjusting her makeup.)*

Flop sweat! And I don't go on for another hour.

> *(JACKIE enters. He is surprised to see JENNIFER.)*

JACKIE
Excuse me. I didn't know anyone was...

JENNIFER
Men's dressing room is across the hall.

JACKIE
Men's? I see. What are you? A singer or a stripper?

JENNIFER
I'm a comic.

JACKIE
A comedienne? Really?

JENNIFER
Really. And these days it's more appropriate to say "comedian" or "comic". I prefer comic.

JACKIE
I prefer stripper.

JENNIFER
Look...

JACKIE
(Staggers slightly)
I'm a little light headed. Do you mind if I have a seat?

JENNIFER
Well... All right. Just don't try any funny business.

JACKIE
(Sits)
We're in a comedy club. What type of business should I try?

JENNIFER
Here. Have some water. You don't look so good.

JACKIE
I get that a lot. Thank you, Miss...

JENNIFER
I'm Jennifer. Jennifer Rasmussen.

JACKIE
That's your stage name?

JENNIFER
That's my given name.

JACKIE
Who the hell gives a comic a name like Jennifer Rassburger?

JENNIFER
Rasmussen! My mother. She didn't know she was naming a comic!

JACKIE
No kidding! A comic needs a name that makes people feel good. Take my name, please. Sorry. Jackie James! Look at all the great comedians. Jackie Mason. Jackie Gleason. Jackie Vernon. Jack E. Leonard.

JENNIFER
Jackie Chan.

JACKIE
It's a global phenomenon!

It's punchy! Staccato! Rat-a-tat-tat!

JENNIFER
Rat-a-tat-tat?! I haven't heard anyone actually say that since my high school did "The Music Man".

JACKIE
I'll bet you were the librarian.

JENNIFER
No. I was the River City hooker. It was a modernist interpretation.

JACKIE
The sadder but wiser girl. As I was saying...

JENNIFER
I like my name. I don't suppose Jackie 'rat-a-tat' James is your real name?

JACKIE
Zalman Schwartz. That's my real name.

JENNIFER
Why'd you change it? (*Laughs*)

JACKIE
What are you, a comedian? My agent at the time, Aaron Solomon, said it sounded too Jewish. Go figure. I was mostly playing the Borscht Belt, and the name didn't stand out. You could run into a half dozen Zalman Schwartz's just going to take a piss at

Grossinger's. I'm sorry about the foul language.

JENNIFER
That's OK. You haven't heard my act.

JACKIE
I never did blue material. Don't believe in it. You shouldn't need to be filthy to be funny.

(He has a coughing fit. Jennifer gets him some more water.)

JENNIFER
It's none of my business, but you might want to see a doctor about that.

JACKIE
I went to the doctor. He gave me six months to live. I said I can't pay you. He gave me another six months.

JENNIFER
Are you OK to go on? Where are you in the lineup?

JACKIE
I usually play for the cleaning crew. Actually, I'm here on other business tonight. I haven't done standup in a while.

JENNIFER
Because of your health?

JACKIE
Because of my act. It stinks. I stopped getting work.

JENNIFER
So change it. You changed your name. Change your act. Maybe it just needs a little polish.

JACKIE
I tried polishing. Turned out I wasn't using Shinola. No, I'm afraid time has passed me by. The younger crowds that come to the clubs these days... they don't want to hear nagging wife jokes, overbearing mother-in-law jokes, or cheap brother-in-law jokes. And they sure as hell don't want to hear ethnic jokes. Except for Jews. You can always make jokes about Jews. And Italians. I have a friend who's half Jewish, half Italian. If he can't get it for your wholesale, he steals it!

(JENNIFER laughs)

JACKIE
Courtesy of my friend and mentor, Jackie Mason.

JENNIFER
People still want jokes about relationships and family. It just needs to come from someplace real. Comedy in your day was just about

delivering one-liners. Now, the important thing is to be inappropriate. Shock value. You have to say things the audience is secretly thinking but would never dare say in public.

JACKIE

What do you know about "my day"? Lenny Bruce. Mort Sahl. Nobody was more inappropriate. It wasn't my style, but they said what they believed. You still have to be able to deliver a punchline. You still need talent. I'll take a Henny Youngman one-liner or a Jack Benny stare any day of the week over some raunchy material about things that are better left private.

JENNIFER

I understand that. The comedians you admired were brilliant! But they came from a different era. It's no different with comics from Lily Tomlin to Tina Fey or Amy Schumer. Or ME! It's not fair to compare. It's like trying to compare great athletes from different generations. Who was the better boxer, Jack Dempsey or Muhammed Ali? What's the point? Enjoy them for what they did when they did it.

JACKIE

You like boxing?

JENNIFER
Yes. I'm not some lightweight, Mr. James.

JACKIE
I like you, Miss Rasputin.

JENNIFER
Rassburger. Rasmussen! Thank you, but you're not my type... yet.

JACKIE
What I mean is...

(He coughs)

JENNIFER
I'm starting to worry about you. Should I call someone? The stage manager? Your mother-in-law?

JACKIE
May she rest in peace, which she never gave me a minute of!

(They BOTH laugh.)

I just want to thank you.

JENNIFER
For what?

JACKIE
For being what I hoped you would be.

JENNIFER
What you hoped I would be? What are you talking about?

JACKIE
Please hear me out. This may sound a little *meshuga*, but I wanted to pass something on to someone. Leave something of myself behind.

JENNIFER
Oh my God! Oh my God! Don't tell me you're some crazy rich guy and you're looking for someone to leave your fortune to!

JACKIE
(*A beat*) No.

JENNIFER
Shit!

Then what is it? What is it you want to leave behind?

JACKIE
My name. Take my name, please.

JENNIFER
You did that joke already. It wasn't funny the first time.

JACKIE
I'm serious! Jackie James! I'm not using it to any great advantage. And it works both ways... male or female.

JENNIFER
Sounds like my ex-husband.

Look. You seem like a sweet old man. But I'm on in 30 minutes. I've got to get my head on straight. We've had a pleasant chat about the good old days. And boxing. I sense that you're developing a crush on me. It happens. What can I say? Are you staying at a retirement home? Maybe I can drop in some time and do 30 minutes.

(JACKIE is obviously hurt by this.)

That was unfeeling. I'm sorry. I'm a little jumpy. I've heard there's someone here tonight from SNL scouting talent. This could be the break I've been waiting for!

JACKIE
I think you've misunderstood me. Thank you anyway. For the water.
(He puts the water back on the dressing table.)
Say, maybe I could put in a good word for you. I used to know people.

JENNIFER
You'd do that for me?

JACKIE
Sure. Why not? I can't promise it will do any good. Hope it isn't someone I owe money to. I'm trying to get my affairs in order. Just getting them in order. Not actually paying anyone back.

JENNIFER
Why are you getting your affairs in order?

JACKIE
My doctor suggested it. I think he secretly wanted to be a lawyer. He should specialize in malpractice.

JENNIFER
I thought you were joking before.

JACKIE
Occupational hazard.

JENNIFER
You're dying?! Are you serious?!

JACKIE
As serious as a heart attack. Sorry. I can't help myself. Look, we all die eventually. I've died a thousand deaths on stage, but facing the real thing. It's different...

JENNIFER
(Starts to cry.)
I can't do this. How the fuck am I supposed to be funny after this?!
(Flipping through her index cards.)
I can't even remember my routine. Jesus Christ!

JACKIE
Here. Have some water.

(She takes a swig.)

JENNIFER
What is going on?

JACKIE
I knew it was a crazy idea. I just thought someone else might have better luck as Jackie James than I had. I came so close. I was booked on Johnny Carson's Tonight Show as a young comedian.

JENNIFER
The Tonight Show?! Oh my God! What happened?

JACKIE
I was doing quite well on the Borscht Belt circuit. Little did I know that I was at the tail end of that era. Jackie Mason kind of took me

under his wing. He saw that things were changing and knew that the only real future for comedians was in television. He mentioned me to Johnny and the next thing I know, my agent gets a call. They want me on the show. So the night I'm scheduled to appear, I'm back there in the green room. Nervous as hell.

There's maybe 20 minutes left of the taping. Then Johnny introduces his next guest, Gore Vidal. Gore Vidal! What the hell is Gore Vidal doing on the Tonight Show?! He belongs on Cavett! Well, the interview ran long and I got bumped. Never heard from them again.

JENNIFER
I'm so sorry. You must have been devastated.

JACKIE
I burned my copy of "Myra Breckinridge". I went into a kind of depression, I guess. A couple of failed marriages. That should have been a comedy gold mine, but I just struck dirt.

JENNIFER
And now you want to pass this tremendous legacy on to me? What did I ever do to you?!

JACKIE
You turned out well.

JENNIFER
I turned out well? We just met, I insulted you, and now you want to bequeath me your name?

JACKIE
Well, when you put it like that, it does sound a little kooky. Miss Rasmussen... may I call you Jennifer?

JENNIFER
That *is* my name.

JACKIE
The truth is...Jennifer...

JENNIFER
I don't have a lot of time.

JACKIE
Neither do I.

JENNIFER
Don't say that.

JACKIE
The truth is... I'm your father.
> (*JENNIFER stares at him in disbelief*)

Did you hear what I said?

JENNIFER
Who are you, really? Is this some sort of joke?

JACKIE
That's what a New York Times critic asked when he saw my act. I'm not joking now. I met your mother in Poughkeepsie. She came to the club where I was working. I spotted her in the audience and had to meet her. One thing led to another, we started living together. Then she told me she was pregnant. I was gone the next day. I'm your father.

JENNIFER
Now I know how Luke Skywalker felt.

JACKIE
I'm sorry.

JENNIFER
Sorry? Who the fuck are you?! I don't believe this! My father?! I *have* a father! He died when I was 10! He loved me as much as any father ever loved a child. And I miss him every day. And you come here with some bullshit story about being my father...

JACKIE
I'm sorry. But it's true. I'm willing to take a paternity test. You have my DNA.

JENNIFER
I've got your DNA right here!

(She spits toward him)

JACKIE
I guess I deserve that.

JENNIFER
Let's say I believe you. Why show up now? I have nothing to give you. And you apparently have nothing for me other than a name.

JACKIE
I don't want anything from you. I know I haven't given you anything, except maybe my comedy gene.

JENNIFER
With my luck, you also gave me your "success" gene.

JACKIE
You clearly got your mother's sarcasm gene. And her looks. I'm glad.

JENNIFER
Please don't talk about my mother. It's really creepy. So now what, *Dad*?!

JACKIE
I just thought you should know your history. I know your mother never told you about me, but didn't you wonder?

JENNIFER
Of course, I wondered. I've spent enough time in therapy wondering why my biological

father had no interest in me. Why were my childhood heroes people like Carol Burnett, Lucille Ball, Joan Rivers? Neither of my parents had much interest in comedy. Now I can understand why my mother never came to see me perform.

JACKIE
I was wrong. After I learned that your mother had the baby... you... I was too ashamed to show my face. I thought once I became a hit, I could come back and be a part of your lives. I never became a hit... your mother married... I'm sorry. I should have stayed away. It was selfish of me. I don't know what got into me this time.

JENNIFER
This time? What do you mean?

JACKIE
I tried to find the nerve to introduce myself a few times before. When I came to see your act.

JENNIFER
You've seen my act?

JACKIE
A few times in the last year.

JENNIFER
That explains why I've been having this recurring dream about a stalker... What do you think? Of my act.

JACKIE
(Hesitates)
Nice.

JENNIFER
Nice? What kind of comment is that? The weather is nice! Puppies are nice! Elevator music is nice! My act is nice?

JACKIE
I mean that in a nice way.

JENNIFER
What's wrong with my act?

JACKIE
Nothing. Nothing. It just makes me a little uncomfortable. That's all.

JENNIFER
Why should my act make you uncomfortable?

JACKIE
Have you noticed that you have a habit of repeating what I say in the form of a question? Were you a contestant on *Jeopardy*?

JENNIFER
It's because nothing I've heard from you makes any sense! You didn't answer my question.

JACKIE
(Reaching for the index cards)
Do you mind?

JENNIFER
(She hesitates then hands him the index cards)
Knock yourself out.

JACKIE
You write your act on index cards?

JENNIFER
Yes. It's modular. I can mix it up depending on my mood. Which right now sucks.

JACKIE
It's not your mood that's important. It's the mood you create for your audience that counts.

(Puts on reading glasses)
No... No... No... No...

JENNIFER
OK. Give them back. What's wrong with this one?

JACKIE
Phone sex?

JENNIFER
(Performing the bit)
I've had a lot of odd jobs. Being a phone sex operator, or as my resume says, Vocal Coach, was probably the oddest. I didn't last long. They said I was rude to the customers. This guy calls and says "I want to be humiliated." I said you just called a phone sex line so you can reach out and touch yourself. I don't know what more I can do for you.

You're supposed to laugh there.

JACKIE
It's embarrassing.

JENNIFER
I can't believe this. You've worked in comedy clubs for decades. God only knows how many women you've impregnated and abandoned over the years. And I'm supposed to believe you're uncomfortable because... why? Because I was a vocal coach?

JACKIE
You're my little girl. How can I be comfortable hearing that?

JENNIFER
No! I may be your daughter, but I'm not your little girl! You didn't change my diapers or give me a bath or play "This Little Piggy". So no, I'm not your little girl. And don't even think of doing any of those things now!

(She assumes a boxer stance)

JACKIE
Whoa! Take it easy, champ. Why would you even say such a thing?

JENNIFER
Well, you did ask me if I was a stripper.

JACKIE
I was just making small talk.

JENNIFER
You must be hell at a party. Nice weather we're having. Would you like to remove your clothing?

JACKIE
I wasn't sure I would go through with it this time. I wanted to talk to you the other times, but I lost my nerve.

JENNIFER
Seems to me you have a lot of nerve. You could afford to lose some.

JACKIE
I know all of this must be a shock to you.

JENNIFER
No. The ending of *Sixth Sense* was a shock. I don't know what this is.

JACKIE
I suppose I could've broken the news to you more gradually. You know, like the old joke where a man leaves his cat with his brother while he goes on vacation. When he comes back, he calls his brother to see when he can pick up the cat. The brother says, "I'm so sorry, but while you were away, the cat died."

The man gets very upset and says, "You know, you could have broken the news to me better than that. When I called the first day, you could have said he was on the roof and won't come down. Then when I called the next day, you could have said that he fell off and the vet was working on patching him up. Then when I called the third day, you could have said he passed away."

The brother thought about it and apologized.

"So how's Mom?" asked the man.

BOTH
"She's on the roof and won't come down."

JENNIFER
(Chuckles)
I've always liked that joke. When did you know you wanted to be a comic?

JACKIE
My bar-mitzvah. I remember standing up there at the bema. Looking out at the crowd. Family, friends, members of the congregation. I had a prepared speech, telling my mother and father how much I appreciated them. But something came over me... Today, I am a man. My mother said that means now I have to remember to put the toilet seat down. Laughter. So I continued... My father said, "I guess now it's time we have a little talk." I said that's not necessary, I already know about sex. He said, "Well maybe you can give me a few pointers." Silence. I had laid my first egg. But instead of giving up I just decided I needed to learn to read my audience a little bit better. Especially if my father is in the audience. How about you?

JENNIFER

Around the same age... junior high. I wasn't the ravishing thing you see before you now. So I became kind of the class clown. I usually played comic roles in class plays. The boys either liked me because I was funny or they were intimidated by me. Either way, I guess I felt empowered. I remember one day in math class the teacher asked me, "What is the value of pi?" I answered "You can serve it hot or cold and share it with your friends." The class cracked up. I got detention, but I was hooked.

JACKIE

The thing that we're meant to be shows up early in life. For us it's laughter. Laughter is what's important in this world. I feel like we're connecting.

JENNIFER

Don't try to force things. I'm not ready for all this.

VOICEOVER AND SOUND OF APPLAUSE

Give it up one more time for Antwan Griffin!!

JENNIFER

That's my cue. I'm up next. It was so great meeting you, Mr. Jackie James.

JACKIE
Jennifer... (*He coughs*)

JENNIFER
Water's on the table. Help yourself.

JACKIE
Will you be all right? (*She doesn't respond*). I'll be going then.

JENNIFER

> (*She starts to exit, comes back to the dressing table and writes something on a piece of note paper. Hands the note to JACKIE*)

Call next time.

> (*She exits*)

JACKIE
I will! I will! Knock 'em dead.

> (*JACKIE sits on the futon. Looks at the note.*)

VOICEOVER
And now let's welcome Jennifer Rasmussen!

> (*Applause*)

JACKIE

Who was it that said, "dying is easy, comedy is hard"? Some dead schmuck, I guess.

(Lights fade on JACKIE and a spot comes up on JENNIFER "on stage". In this next sequence, both JENNIFER and JACKIE are performing. The spot alternates between the two.)

JENNIFER

So, how are you this evening? Good? Good. Good. I've had a miserable day, so I'm glad someone is happy. You're already feeling good and yet you came to listen to some mental wreck make you feel even better? How crazy is that? I've been in some crazy relationships. Relationships are so difficult... (*SHE hesitates*)

I met my father this evening. I mean met for the very first time. My biological father. I had a father growing up. A man who took responsibility for someone else's mistake. Turns out my "real" father is a comedian. Not that you would've heard of him. He's not exactly a household name, even in his own household.

(A second spot comes up on JACKIE "on stage". He seems more in his prime then our last image of him.)

JACKIE

Good evening drunks, dieters, and debtors! It's great to be here in (*choose a city*). I don't want to say the police are aggressive here, but I got a parking ticket at the McDonald's drive through. I was recently married. Thank you. Thank you. Even more recently divorced. Thank you very much. For our honeymoon, my wife wanted to go to a foreign locale. Someplace secluded. I took her to Chernobyl. What a waste! Get it? Waste? Anybody out there?

JENNIFER

How should I describe him? He's kind of a cross between Woody Allen and Johnny Appleseed. A kindly looking Jewish man who travels around planting his seed. But he never looks back to see the beautiful apple tree that sprung up. That would be me in case you were having trouble following my train of thought. Did you hear that Woody Allen and Roman Polanski are teaming up on a remake of *Rosemary's Baby*? They're calling it *Rosemary's Baby 2... Young.*

JACKIE

I never know the right things to say to a woman. I went shopping with my wife. Big mistake. She tried on a pair of jeans and said,

"Do these jeans make me look fat?" I said no! The *jeans* don't make you look fat. And her father is something else. His first wife passed away, and he's now planning to marry his high school sweetheart. Imagine that. She graduates next year.

JENNIFER

My father is dying. My biological father. The father who raised me, died when I was 10. I've never thought much of death. Not all that crazy about *life* at the moment. If there's a heaven, I'm hoping that's where I end up. I imagine it in the traditional way... you know, pearly gates, St. Peter there to welcome you. Or check IDs. Maybe they have bouncers in case someone tries to avoid an eternity of damnation. Like for abandoning their kid. I'm sorry. Maybe I'm sharing too much too soon. The father who raised me is on the roof, and my biological father is climbing up to bring him down...

JACKIE

How many of you have ever been in trouble with the law? That many? I could tell you were a tough crowd as soon as I walked out. I had a legal problem once. I'll spare you the details. I asked my brother-in-law to represent me. He said "the judge has issued a *subpoena duces tecum*". What about my *tuchus*?! "It means you have to provide evidence. The judge also issued a *subpoena ad testificandum*. That means you have to testify orally." If I have to testify *orally*, why do I need a condom?!

Thank you. If I can be serious for a moment. I'd like to share something a little personal. I have a child. A daughter. Somewhere. To say I was an absent father would be like saying Bernie Madoff was a little greedy. I failed at the most important job in my life. What happens here onstage maybe isn't so critical. But you know, they say that laughter is the best medicine. And he who laughs last, laughs best. So if I've provided a few laughs and in some small way helped ease someone's pain, then perhaps I haven't lived my life as a complete *putz*!

> *(He starts to sing September Song. At the end there is a blackout on JACKIE)*

JENNIFER

I should've started with the cat.

The truth is, deep down I wanted this day to come. I wanted to know this man. Maybe I wanted him to be something different. Maybe I already see too much of myself in him.

What do I do now? Do I just forgive him and try to forget all the pain he's caused? Isn't that what the aggrieved party is supposed to do? I don't know. He doesn't deserve it, but I want to know more. I want to know who my grandparents were. Do I have uncles, aunts, cousins I've never heard of? Maybe it's better that way. Who knows? But I'd like to know. When I go to the doctor, there's an entire half of me that has no family history. I'm allergic to dogs. Is that because of him? You've been awfully quiet.

Umm... I was told there was a talent scout from SNL here tonight. Sorry to disappoint. Please give my best to Lorne. Mr. Michaels. Guess I'll follow the family tradition of having a close brush with fame.

The other acts were great though, weren't they? I predict big things for Antwan. I think my time is up. Thank you all for listening. I should be paying you instead of my psychiatrist. You've been a lovely audience. I'm Jennifer... I'm Jennifer... I'm Jackie James! Good night!

(Blackout.)

{Music: Jimmy Durante singing "September Song"}

Late Nights in Cars

By

Michael Gilles

Cast of Characters

EMILY   Daddy's Daughter, ages 0 to 30

DADDY   Ages 36 to 66

Scene

In and around a series of cars and the space between a father and daughter.

Time

1987 through 2017

Act I Scene 1

Setting:: Two chairs, representing a series of cars.

At Rise:: DADDY and EMILY are seated in a car facing the audience. DADDY is behind the wheel

(Note: The characters move constantly throughout the play, sometimes one or both sitting in the car, other times wandering in open space. They do not touch throughout.)

EMILY

I first met Daddy when I was three minutes old. It was down a hall, through a door, in a hollow glass basket. His face was six inches from mine.

(Daddy steps from the car and walking toward the audience. He leans over as if he's coming face to face with his daughter for the first time. He sings a lullaby.)

DADDY

Hush-a-bye
Don't you cry
Go to sleepy little baby
When you wake
You shall have
All the pretty little horses

Blacks and bays
Dapples and greys
All the pretty little horses

When you wake
You shall have
All the pretty little horses

> *(He pauses, then looks at the baby, beaming.)*

I think we'll call you Emily.

and as the curtains catch
the slight spring morning air
i see angels dancing on the sill
and i thank God for you
and this the sweetest gift
i see the world anew
through your eyes

> *(DADDY continues.)*

The C4 Corvette. Best handling car ever. 230 horsepower, tuned-port fuel injected L98 5.7-liter 350 V-8 engine. Leather sport seats. Delco-Bilstein shock absorbers. Delco-Bose stereo system. Zero to 30: 2.4 seconds. Zero to 60: 5.7 seconds. Zero to 100: 22.3 seconds. Top speed? 150 miles per hour, although I never made it that high. Bright red.

America's most beloved sports car.

> *(EMILY is a baby and shrieks and cries because DADDY has stopped the car.)*

Now...a station wagon...4 wheels...looks like shit.

> *(She cries again. To her, cooing.)*

It's alright, sweet pea, it's alright. Daddy loves driving you around in a large, safe, piece of crap.

EMILY

My first real memories took place in our car. Not a station wagon; no, not THE station wagon. Ford Taurus. "Best selling car in the US of A", Dad would say.

DADDY

I actually loved that car. Best selling car in the US of A. Looked like a flying potato...and I mean that as a compliment. Front-wheel drive. Aerodynamic design. V6 engine. Like sitting in a cockpit. I tell you, when we got that car...the old wagon smelled like it looked, but the Taurus and that new car smell...

EMILY
(Matter of fact, almost with pride.)
Daddy, Daddy, I pooped my pants!

(DADDY hangs his head, defeated.)

DADDY
Soon after the poop, not because of the poop, of course, Mom and I moved...took a lot of stuff, but the only important things were Emily, and the Taurus.

We moved to a newer, bigger neighborhood, for Emily's sake. So she would have friends her age. A cooler neighborhood. Not cool as in "hey, look at us, we're cool", or "hey look at us, we're freezing". No, cool as in cold, and mean, and crushing to a little girl.

(EMILY looks off into the distance.)

My first memory of the little girls in the neighborhood, those cold, mean girls, was the first neighborhood Easter egg hunt. Obnoxious, flipping their hair at Emily, then turning their backs on her, then smirking and running away from her, just to be mean. Emily, of course, was crushed; cried all the way home.

(EMILY cries.)

All I could say to her was, "bullies are boring, and nice kids are interesting. You know what I'm saying, right? That makes you interesting".

> *(EMILY stops crying.)*

She stopped crying, soaking up my words of wisdom. But I was on a roll...

> *(He gets excited and blurts out...)*

Let's egg their houses!!!!

And we did, embarrassingly enough.

The next time, the worst time they hurt her...I looked out the window one day and saw her standing on the very end of our lawn, staring across the street at the mean girls, motionless, just staring. Her pain shot through me like an arrow.

All I could do was call her over to me. I leaned over, put my hands on her shoulders, and whispered...

"Let's get ice cream!".

And we drove off in our Taurus, driving way too fast to the nearest Dairy Queen. She got a cone, I got satisfaction. As we passed the mean girls on the way back, I told her to wave her ice cream out the window. Then I yelled "BITCHES!!!"

Well, of course, I didn't do the last part. But I thought it.

EMILY
I think that was my favorite moment growing up. At that moment, Daddy became my awesome hero. And thus began our love affair with early mornings in cars, mid-afternoons in cars, and late nights in cars.

DADDY
So, Charlie Brown, what did my cute little fourth grader do at school today?

EMILY
I fell asleep in math class.

DADDY
Mm hmmm.

EMILY
I fell asleep outside geography class.

DADDY
Mm hmmm.

EMILY
I fell asleep during recess.

DADDY
Mm hmmm.

EMILY

I smushed a piece of pizza all over Sarah Solberg's sweater during lunch.

DADDY

Mm hmmm. Wait, what?

EMILY

At least I didn't sleep the whole day long!

DADDY

(Into phone.)

Sooo...Mr. Solberg. I, um, hear that your daughter's sweater looked a little different when she got home tonight. No, you're right, not funny.

(Transition.)

After an interesting roller coaster ride through grade school, Emily settled down some. Just some. No more sweater smushings. Just an interesting ride.

Then came the Toyota Sienna. A big car, a minivan, a soccer mom's car. I guess that made me a soccer dad. It was good though, halfway between a pickup truck, which I really wanted, and a Beetle, which I couldn't fit in. But it took us on our rides, those long trips at night that quieted our hearts and relaxed our souls.

EMILY

It was junior high when I first began playing music for Dad. It was stuff he didn't know at all...Rage Against the Machine, Kasabian, Red Hot Chili Peppers. He said he knew their stuff, but I could tell he was lying. I knew he was lying, because about the same time, he started wearing cotton in his ears.

DADDY

That was a very special time for me. Not so much the music, although I eventually became cool and actually liked it. It was the late nights driving through cornfields, lit only by our headlights and the moon and the stars. Sometimes, we would turn off the headlights and drive in the dark. I loved that. I think it scared the shit out of Emily.

EMILY

Oh yes.

(Transition.)

I think by high school, I had Dad convinced that he would never again hear classic rock in his car. I introduced him to Death Cab for Cutie...

DADDY

Uhhh...what?

EMILY
Death Cab for Cutie. What's wrong with that?

DADDY
One, I think you're lying. There can't be a band name Death Cab for Cutie. Second of all, in my day, bands had normal names.

EMILY
Like the Bonzo Dog Doo-Dah Band?

DADDY
Get out. In all my years there has never been a band called the Bonzo...that name.

EMILY
Death Cab for Cutie was named after the song Death Cab for Cutie performed by the Bonzo Dog Doo-Dah Band. It was in the Magical Mystery Tour.

You know, the Beatles movie? The classic rock Beatles movie?

DADDY
Show off.

(Transition.)

So, high school began a new stage of my relationship with Emily. We began to share our secrets, swearing to never tell a living soul about our private thoughts and deeds.

(After stammering for a minute.)

I tried marijuana a few times.

EMILY

Are you kidding? Weed is, like, my favorite hobby!

DADDY

Oh dear God.

(More stammering.)

I cheated on a test once.

EMILY

I would pay Mary Cappelli to take my Calculus tests for me. She and I would move our desks just slightly enough so I could see her paper. That's why I got A's all year. I mean, I couldn't even spell Calculus, never mind understand it.

DADDY

(Moaning.)

Why am I doing this?

EMILY

I lost my virginity at the Dancing Pins Bowling Alley. We used to call it the balling alley.

DADDY

(Panicked. Reaches for CD player.)

Oh no God!!! Quick!!! Death Cab for Cutie!!!

EMILY

It was in 11th grade that everything changed. Mom died.

DADDY

Lovely girl, Mom didn't...

EMILY

...make it. She had a bad heart. Finally, it caught up with her and yanked her away from us. It changed Dad. It changed me too. We would still go on our rides, listening to my, our, music, but it was more to salve the nasty noise in our heads.

EMILY

Dad, I got in.

DADDY

Where?

EMILY

Dickinson. I'm so sorry...it's three hours away.

DADDY

Why are you sorry? This is great news!

EMILY

Well. With Mom gone, I just...

DADDY

Hell. Three hours ain't nothing.

(She laughs.)

EMILY
I love you, Dad.

DADDY
I love you too, Charlie Brown.

(Transition.)

So, college. Emily was right. I was afraid to be alone. So I would visit her, two, three times a week. It was only three hours away. Well, six, really, if you count the whole round-trip thing. All we would do is drive in and around the countryside around school, talking and laughing and listening to music until all that was left was the music and the sweet silence of the night. Then I would go home. And at five in the morning I would get out of the car, stand in my driveway, and gaze at the stars looking to fall asleep, and feeling content, and at peace, because my daughter was still in my life.

EMILY
Soon after I graduated, I moved home, not much more than five miles from Dad's house. And my life changed, for the good. I got married. My man was perfect in every way, except one. He didn't like to go on rides. He would always say, "it's boring, and your music is terrifying." So Dad and I still had that, the rides, the music, the talks, the peace at night.

(Transition.)
Dad, I still miss her so much.

DADDY
I know you do. So do I.

EMILY
If I only had her back, just for a moment...I never had a chance to say goodbye.

DADDY
My sweet little Emily, there aren't enough goodbyes in the universe that would make it any easier. But you've moved on. Life is good. You have a husband who's a good man, a home that's not only warm and loving, but a short ride to your awesome dad's house. You have love, and will, God willing, have a child. So I can have a grandson.

EMILY
A grandson, huh! You don't want another me in your life?

DADDY
Lord no.

(Transition.)

EMILY
I don't know how he managed it, but sure enough, it was a son.

DADDY

I think we'll call you...

EMILY

Winston...

DADDY

(Frowns in disdain. Then back to the baby.)

Billy.

EMILY

(Frowns back. Then with disdain.)

Billy.

And everything was good for a while. My husband was good to me, Billy was a charmer, and Dad was the best granddad ever. Billy called him not Pop-Pop, not grandpa, but Ohno. Dad would come up behind him and in a booming voice and say...

DADDY

Helloooooo my boy.

EMILY

And Billy would hear that voice and curl up and shout "OH NO". And it stuck. Which of course, delighted Dad to no end.

Then one day, out of nowhere...

DADDY
You're very pretty.

EMILY
Why thank you.

DADDY
(After a pause.)
Who are you?

EMILY
I guess I didn't realize it at the time, but at that moment, my life changed forever. On our drives, I would be the driver. In the dim confines of his home, I would be the light. I would drive.

At first, it wasn't too bad. Dad would lose something or forget the names of places or things. Heck, I do that. It just wasn't a big deal.

Then he would repeat himself a lot, or forget why he was doing something.

DADDY
Charlie Brown, why don't you ever call me?

EMILY
Dad, I just left you. We had a nice conversation.

DADDY
Yes. Ok. I remember that. What did we talk about? Are you sure you were here? You could have been at your brother's. He looks like me.

EMILY
Dad, I don't have a brother.

DADDY
Well there's no reason to get snippy with me.
(Transition.)
I know I'm sick. It's like a veil that I can't quite see through, then laughter, or sadness, will flick on a memory, and I can see past the veil and into my life.
(With pen and paper in hand.)
Emily, I want you to remember me. I want you to remember me the way I was. I want you to know that I listened to every word you said, and loved you no matter what you said. That every moment was the best.

EMILY
Read it to me, Dad.

DADDY
We would drive all night...

EMILY

And?

DADDY

That's all I got.

(They have a laugh together. He goes back behind his veil.)

EMILY

Then, he began to talk on and on about things, repeating the same stories over and over again.

DADDY

I remember the Navy days. They were the best. Coming home in my flight suit. You and Billy waiting for gifts. Yep, your old dad was really something.

EMILY

Dad, you weren't in the Navy. That was Grandpa. And Billy is your grandson.

DADDY

Yes. Ok. I remember that. But those really were good days. Your grandpa and me on a ship in our uniforms. Looking crisp. It's a shame that you and Billy didn't sign up. Then the four of us would be together, on a boat, no, on a ship. No, where was it...

EMILY
I really didn't mind, though. It meant that I could still talk with him, and hear his laugh. And most of the time he still knew who I was. He'd still call me Charlie Brown, and love the nighttime rides in my Toyota, and complain when we had to go home. At least, he knew who I was.

DADDY
Girl?

EMILY
Dad, I'm Emily, your daughter.

DADDY
I think we'll call you...girl.

EMILY
Well, it turns out that he really didn't know who I was. I was sometimes Mom, sometimes Grandma, sometimes the brother I didn't have.

(Transition.)
We were out in our car, driving late at night, finding comfort in the quiet and the moonlit fields. We were on Robinsonville near Conley Church when a sudden movement pulled me from the pain and anger of my inner thoughts. In the bright glow of our headlights stood a deer, too old to be a doe, but somewhere nearer to the end of her life. She had begun to

sprint across the road, but something made her stop suddenly, and we did the same.

DADDY
Damn deer almost broke my car.

EMILY
And we stared at each other, she and I. In my eyes, she could see relief at a calamity averted. That is, if this creature cared a whit about my eyes. No, the more fascinating look was in her eyes. It was arrogance, no, defiance. Defiance, as if to say, "No, not now, not in this place. I will choose when and where I die, and it will not be on this cool autumn evening, on this road, by your hand. My death will have dignity, if for no other reason than I will know when it comes, and I will embrace the chance to give myself back to the earth. But not now, not in this place."

Dignity.

DADDY
Girl? Girl??? I pooped my pants.

(EMILY cries softly.)

(Transition.)

(EMILY picks up cell phone.)

EMILY

Hello? It's three o'clock in the morning. Who is this? Oh my God, no. I'll be right there.

DADDY

(Flailing around at unseen policeman.)

Get away from me you son of a bitch. I have to get to work. Let me go, or I'll kill you. I can't be late. I have to get to work.

EMILY

Dad, dad. It's three o'clock in the morning. I'll get you to work in the morning. I promise. It's alright. It's alright. Shh, shh. It's alright.

(Transition.)

I was exhausted, and afraid. Afraid that he would die, afraid that he would hurt me, afraid that I would hurt him. I couldn't breathe. I felt so afraid, so angry, and so guilty. I loved him with all my heart. How could it end this way?

DADDY

(Writing.)

We would drive all night. We would drive all night. We would drive all night.

(He throws pad and begins to sob.)

I don't want this.

(To EMILY.)
I...don't...know...who...you...are.

EMILY
A few weeks later, we were on one of our beloved car rides when my awesome hero did the most amazing thing.

DADDY
(He leans forward.)
Hush-a-bye
Don't you cry
Go to sleepy little baby
When you wake
You shall have
All the pretty little horses

Blacks and bays
Dapples and greys
All the pretty little horses

When you wake
You shall have
All the pretty little horses

I think we'll call you...Emily.

Ah, my lovely girl. My Emily.

EMILY
Then he died.

(She leans toward him and kisses him on the head. It is the first time they have touched in the play. After a pause...)

Goodbye, daddy.

(She turns upstage.)

(DADDY stands up, his old self. He moves forward and recites completed Late Nights in Cars.)

DADDY

We would drive all night
> *(Pause.)*

Through corn fields lit only
By the stars and headlights,
Ours, on untended roads
With ancient names like
Indian Mission
Beaver Dam, alone
Except for the lost deer,

Finding its way much
Like us, on a search
Yearning for a path
For home.

She'd play music, my
Girl, orchestrating
Rare symphonies for

The lone white birch and
For the otherwise silent
Ponds and fields ahead
Her songs calming the
Terrible screaming
In my head til we'd
Pass old Harbeson
Cemetery to Cave Neck
And home.

> *(He pauses. Then, approving...)*

Huh.

(He moves back and turns upstage.)

THE END

Acknowledgements

Generations opened August 2, 2019, at Colonial Players in Annapolis, Maryland.

Monuments was directed by Lois Evans and starred Jeffrey Miller and Kate Wheeler.

Last Laugh was directed by Rick Wade and starred Robin Schwartz and Jerry Vess

Late Nights in Cars was directed by Frank Moorman and starred Jim Reiter and Erica Miller.

The playwrights are deeply grateful to Colonial Players and all who made this production so fulfilling.

About the Playwrights

Stephen Evans, Morey Norkin, and Michael Gilles have been friends since high school, performing with and for one another and eventually founding a theater company together. With *Generations*, their nearly fifty-year partnership (now distanced in location though not in laughter) has found a new path, for and on which they are truly grateful.

Lightning Source UK Ltd.
Milton Keynes UK
UKHW011018210820
368606UK00002B/306